BECOMING A
contagious christian

YOUTH EDITION

BECOMING A

contagious christian

COMMUNICATING YOUR FAITH IN A STYLE THAT FITS YOU

ZONDERVAN™

GRAND RAPIDS, MICHIGAN 49530

WILLOW CREEK RESOURCES

ARK MITTELBERG | LEE STROBEL | BILL HYBELS

REVISED AND EXPANDED FOR STUDENTS BY **BO BOSHERS**

We want to hear from you. Please send your comments about this book to us in care of the address below. Thank you.

GRAND RAPIDS, MICHIGAN 49530

w w w . z o n d e r v a n . c o m

ZONDERVAN™

Becoming a Contagious Christian Youth Edition Student's Guide
Copyright © 2001 by the Willow Creek Association

Requests for information should be addressed to:

Zondervan, *Grand Rapids, Michigan 49530*

ISBN 0-310-23773-4

All Scripture quotations, unless otherwise indicated, are taken from the *Holy Bible: New International Version®*. NIV®. Copyright © 1973, 1978, 1984 by International Bible Society. Used by permission of Zondervan. All rights reserved.

Scripture quotations marked NLT are taken from the *Holy Bible,* New Living Translation, copyright © 1996. Used by permission of Tyndale House Publishers, Inc., Wheaton, IL 60189. All rights reserved.

Interior design by Rob Monacelli

Printed in the United States of America

01 02 03 04 05 06 07 / ❖ DC/ 12 11 10 9 8 7

This project is dedicated to the junior and senior high students whose compassion for lost friends motivates them to reach out to and lead their generation to Christ, one life at a time.

My prayer is that you, a student in this course, will realize how God wants to use you to be a difference-maker on your school campus and in every area of your life. You have the truth and the hope your friends are looking for. I pray that the training you receive will give you the boldness and confidence to never feel ashamed, afraid, or unprepared to share the greatest news of all—Jesus is our Savior and King.

This project is also dedicated to the youth leaders who will teach this course to students. My prayer is that God will use you in a powerful way, not only with the words you speak but with the life you lead, so students can both hear and see what being a contagious Christian is all about.

BO BOSHERS

contents

why become
a contagious christian?

PREVIEW

Session 1 you will:

- Discover the myths about evangelism and evangelists

- Learn what relational evangelism really is

- Discover what the Bible says about sharing our faith

- Begin an *Impact List* of people you want to share Christ's love with

stereotypes of evangelists

Negative	Positive

what is relational evangelism?

1. REAL

2. _____

3. _____

4. VERBAL

"How can they believe in the one of whom they have not heard? And how can they hear without someone preaching to them?" (Romans 10:14)

5. _____

6. TEAM-ORIENTED

"A person's coming to Christ is like a chain with many links. There is the first link, middle links, and a last link. There are many influences and conversations that precede a person's decision to convert to Christ. I know the joy of being the first link at times, a middle link usually, and occasionally the last link. God has not called me to only be the last link. He has called me to be faithful and to love all people."*

7. "PUTTING OTHERS FIRST"

*Cliff Knechtle, *Give Me an Answer*, InterVarsity Press, 1986.

video vignette:
lost and found

1. As you watch the video, look for reasons why you would want to become a contagious Christian.

2. List the reasons in the space provided.

_____

_____

_____

_____

_____

_____

_____

_____

_____

_____

_____

_____

_____

_____

_____

begin an *impact list*

Most of us have friends or family who don't have a personal relationship with Jesus. Think about people in your life who could use some help in taking the next step in their spiritual lives. Write the names you come up with in the space below.

_____

_____

_____

_____

_____

_____

_____

It's important to remember that your friends are not projects. The purpose of putting names on this list is to help you be more intentional about building stronger relationships with these friends. Your friends need to know that they matter to you because they are your friends, not because you want to convert them. Let them know by the way you act and the things you say that they matter to you—whether or not they agree with the gospel message.

Check your list from time to time. The names will need to change as people move in and out of your life or become Christians. Keeping the list updated will help you stay focused and help keep your prayer support current and strong for each friend on the list.

talk with God about the people on your *impact list*

Begin to pray for the people on your *Impact List*. Ask God to work in their lives and to give you wisdom on how to effectively reach out to them. Here are three areas to talk to God about:

Friends and Family

God, help my friends to . . .

- See how empty life is without you
- Understand why they need your forgiveness
- Break through any confusion they have about Christ
- Recognize how a relationship with Christ could change their life
- Open their hearts to your love and their minds to your truth

You

God, help me to . . .

- Live the kind of life that will make my friends interested in Christ
- Be honest and real in how I deal with the good things and the hard things in my life
- Be a caring friend
- Know what to say to my friends and when and how to say it
- Be prepared to listen to my friends' questions about the Christian life and help them find answers.
- Be bold in telling them about you
- Be willing to be used by you to lead them into a relationship with Christ

Your Relationship with Your Friend

God, help us to . . .

- Build a friendship based on trust and understanding
- Be open to talking about spiritual things
- Keep the friendship strong even if we don't agree about the Christian faith

preview of things to come

OUR GOAL
To become contagious Christians!
Contagious Christians live authentic Christian lives
and tell friends and family about Christ
in a natural and compelling way.

individual assignment:
evangelism styles questionnaire

Directions

1. Fill in the blanks for all 36 statements according to whether you think the statement applies to you:

    3   very much

    2   somewhat

    1   very little

    0   not at all

2. Transfer your responses to the grid on page 18.

3. Add up each column and write the total in the box at the bottom.

_____ 1. I like to say what's on my mind when I talk to people, without a lot of small talk.

_____ 2. I try to learn as much as possible from books and the Internet about controversial issues or important things that are going on in the world.

_____ 3. I often use experiences from my own life to illustrate a point I am trying to make.

_____ 4. I'm a "people person" who believes that friendship is one of the most important things in life.

_____ 5. When I make plans to do something, I really like including new people.

_____ 6. I see needs in people's lives that others usually overlook.

_____ 7. I don't mind making people feel uncomfortable or putting them on the spot during a conversation, if necessary.

_____ 8. I like to analyze things and think through issues.

_____ 9. I often identify with others by saying things like, "I've felt that way too."

_____ 10. People tell me that it's very easy for me to make new friends.

_____ 11. Even if I know the answers, I'm more comfortable having someone who knows more than I do explain Christianity to my friends.

_____ 12. Helping other people makes me feel closer to God.

_____ 13. I believe in being completely truthful with my friends, even if the truth could hurt the friendship.

individual assignment:
evangelism styles questionnaire

_____ 14. I like to ask people challenging questions about their beliefs and opinions.

_____ 15. When I talk about how I became a Christian, I've found that people are interested in my story.

_____ 16. I would rather talk about things that are going on in a person's life than the details of their religious background.

_____ 17. If I knew of a good Christian outreach event that my friends could relate to, I'd really work hard to get them to come.

_____ 18. I'm better at showing love through my actions than through my words.

_____ 19. I believe that if you really love someone, you have to tell that person the truth, even when it's painful.

_____ 20. I enjoy talking about controversial issues and debating tough questions.

_____ 21. I tell people about the mistakes I've made when I think it will help them avoid those same mistakes and relate to the solutions I've found.

_____ 22. I'd rather talk about a person's life before getting into a discussion about their beliefs.

_____ 23. I look for Christian concerts and events to invite my friends to.

_____ 24. I believe that showing people Christian love through my actions will make them more likely to listen to what I have to say.

_____ 25. I believe it's better to risk making a mess of things than it is to do nothing at all.

_____ 26. I get frustrated with people who use weak arguments to explain what they believe.

_____ 27. People seem interested in hearing stories about things that have happened in my life.

_____ 28. I enjoy having long talks with my friends.

_____ 29. When I see, hear, or read something I really like, the first thing I think of is other people I know who would enjoy it or get something out of it too.

_____ 30. I would prefer doing something practical to help someone rather than getting into a religious discussion with them.

_____ 31. I sometimes get into trouble for not being gentle or sensitive in the way I deal with people.

_____ 32. I like to find out the deeper reasons why people believe the things they do.

individual assignment:
evangelism styles questionnaire

_____ 33. Thinking about what God has done in my life really makes me want to tell others about it.

_____ 34. People think of me as a friendly, sensitive, and caring person.

_____ 35. It would be one of the highlights of my week if a friend accepted an invitation to a Christian event.

_____ 36. I'm more practical than philosophical—better with actions than ideas.

Confrontational	Intellectual	Testimonial	Interpersonal	Invitational	Serving
#1 ____	#2 ____	#3 ____	#4 ____	#5 ____	#6 ____
#7 ____	#8 ____	#9 ____	#10 ____	#11 ____	#12 ____
#13 ____	#14 ____	#15 ____	#16 ____	#17 ____	#18 ____
#19 ____	#20 ____	#21 ____	#22 ____	#23 ____	#24 ____
#25 ____	#26 ____	#27 ____	#28 ____	#29 ____	#30 ____
#31 ____	#32 ____	#33 ____	#34 ____	#35 ____	#36 ____
Totals					

being yourself

PREVIEW

Session 2 you will:

- Discover your evangelism style

- Identify a step to develop your evangelism style

- Clarify your evangelism style using the *Evangelism Styles Assessment*

six styles of evangelism

Confrontational Style

Biblical Example:

- _____ in _____

Characteristics:

- Confident

- Assertive

- _____

Cautions:

- When you confront people with the truth, be sensitive to their feelings. If you push too hard, you might turn them off.

six styles of evangelism

Intellectual Style

Biblical Example:

• _____ in _____

Characteristics:

• Curious

• Analytical—put a lot of thought into what to say, do, and believe

• Approach things in a _____ way

Cautions:

• Don't mistake giving people answers for telling them about Christ. Give reasons and evidence, but remember the goal is to be their friend and look for ways to help them trust Christ, not to win a debate.

• Be careful of getting into arguments. You don't want to unnecessarily put up walls between yourself and your friend.

six styles of evangelism

Testimonial Style

Biblical Example:

- _____ in _____

Characteristics:

- Clear communicators

- Interesting storytellers

- _____

Cautions:

- Make sure you tell your story in a way that relates to other people's lives. In order to do that, you first need to *listen* and then relate your story to their situation.

six styles of evangelism

Interpersonal Style

Biblical Example:

- _____ in _____

Characteristics:

- Warm personalities

- Comfortable in conversations

- _____

Cautions:

- Make sure your priorities are straight. Friendships are important, but so is the truth. Sharing Christ with someone challenges their whole direction in life, and that can cause some friction in your relationship. That's a risk we must be willing to take.

six styles of evangelism

Invitational Style

Biblical Example:

- _____ in _____

Characteristics:

- Quick to include others in their activities

- Hospitable

- _____

Cautions:

- Don't let others always do the talking for you. You, too, need to be prepared to share Christ's love. And don't assume your job is done when the people you invite show up at church or a Christian event. Ask them what they thought of the event and look for opportunities to start a spiritual conversation.

six styles of evangelism

Serving Style

Biblical Example:

- _____ in _____

Characteristics:

- Others-centered

- Humble

- _____

Cautions:

- Don't let your actions do all of the talking for you. You need to ver-bally tell people about Christ. Just as words are no substitute for actions, actions are no substitute for words.

- Don't underestimate the value of your service. Your evangelism style will reach people who might not respond to any other style. Acts of loving service are hard to resist and difficult to argue with—even for the most negative and hard-hearted of people.

individual activity:
evangelism styles assessment

Directions

1. Find your personal evangelism style—the one that scored highest on the questionnaire you filled out—in the *Evangelism Styles Assessment* on pages 27–32.

2. Read the information about your evangelism style and check any item you think applies to you. If only a few of the items seem to apply to you, take a look at the style that had the second highest total on your *Evangelism Styles Questionnaire* on page 18. See if that is a better match.

3. Choose one idea to begin working on in order to develop your evangelism style.

4. Write your evangelism style or styles on your *Impact List* on page 120.

Note: If you scored high in more than one style, it may mean you can share your faith through multiple styles, depending on the situation. As you try out different styles, you may find that one or two of them feel more comfortable to you than the others.

confrontational style

Biblical Example: Peter in Acts 2
Theme Verse: 2 Timothy 4:2

> *Preach the word of God. Be persistent, whether the time is favorable or not. Patiently correct, rebuke, and encourage your people with good teaching.* (NLT)

Personal Characteristics:

- ❑ Confident
- ❑ Assertive
- ❑ Direct
- ❑ Bold
- ❑ Skips small talk; likes to get right to the point
- ❑ Has strong opinions and beliefs

Cautions:

- Ask God to help you be sensitive and tactful when you talk to your friends.
- Allow the Holy Spirit to restrain your desire to come on strong in every situation.
- Avoid judging people who approach evangelism with a different style.

Suggestions for Developing and Using This Style:

- ❑ Ask your friends to tell you whether or not you have the right balance of boldness and gentleness. Remind yourself of Paul's expression in Ephesians 4, "speaking the truth in love." Remember, both truth and love are important.
- ❑ Be prepared for situations where you will stand alone in sharing Christ. Under God's guidance challenge people to trust and follow Christ. God will use your boldness.
- ❑ Learn how to ask good, direct questions that help you understand your friend's point of view.
- ❑ Practice "Putting Others First." Listen to what your friends say before you tell them what you think they need to hear.
- ❑ Team up with friends who have other styles that may be better matched to the personality of the person you want to reach.
- ❑ Other: _____

intellectual style

Biblical Example: Paul in Acts 17
Theme Verse: 2 Corinthians 10:5

> *With these weapons we break down every proud argument that keeps people from knowing God. With these weapons we conquer their rebellious ideas, and we teach them to obey Christ.* (NLT)

Personal Characteristics:

❑ Curious—asks a lot of questions
❑ Analytical—puts a lot of thought into what they say, do, and believe
❑ Logical—approaches decisions by thinking through them methodically
❑ Likes to debate
❑ More concerned with what people think than with how they feel

Cautions:

• Avoid letting discussions become heated arguments.
• Remember that attitude is as important as information. First Peter 3:15 reminds us to give an answer with "gentleness and respect."
• Avoid getting sidetracked by issues and arguments, so you can keep the conversation focused on the gospel message.

Suggestions for Developing and Using This Style:

❑ Set aside time to study and prepare. Preparation is very important for this style. Take the words of 1 Peter 3:15 to heart:

> *But in your hearts set apart Christ as Lord. Always be prepared to give an answer to everyone who asks you to give the reason for the hope that you have. But do this with gentleness and respect.*

❑ Get out and talk to people. Try out your reasoning and answers with your friends. Find out what works and what doesn't work and make adjustments based on what you learn.
❑ Be careful not to always focus on intellectual discussions. Talk to your friends about everyday events as well. Find out what's happening in their lives and tell them what's happening in yours.
❑ Team up with friends who have other styles that may be better matched to the personality of the person you want to reach.
❑ Other: _____

testimonial style

Biblical Example: The blind man in John 9
Theme Verse: 1 John 1:3a

> *We proclaim to you what we have seen and heard, so that you also may have fellowship with us.*

Personal Characteristics:

- ❏ Clear communicator
- ❏ Interesting storyteller
- ❏ Good listener
- ❏ Open and honest about personal ups and downs
- ❏ Amazed by how God has extended grace and forgiveness
- ❏ Able to see connections between their own experience and the experiences of others

Cautions:

- Be sure to relate your story to your friend's life. In order to do this, you have to first be a good listener and get to know about them.
- Be careful not to tell your story and leave it at that. Challenge your friend to think about how your experiences might apply to their life.
- Don't downplay your story because you think it's too ordinary. The ordinary story is the kind that relates best to ordinary people.

Suggestions for Developing and Using This Style:

- ❏ Know your story so you will be able to tell it without hesitating.
- ❏ Keep Christ at the center of your story and stay focused on how he changed your life.
- ❏ Keep your story fresh by adding new illustrations about how God is at work in your life.
- ❏ Team up with friends who have other styles that may be better matched to the personality of the person you want to reach.
- ❏ Other: _____

interpersonal style

Biblical Example: Matthew in Luke 5
Theme Verse: 1 Corinthians 9:22b

> *Yes, I try to find common ground with everyone so that I might bring them to Christ.* (NLT)

Personal Characteristics:

❏ Warm personality
❏ Comfortable in conversations
❏ Friendship-oriented
❏ Compassionate—sympathetic when someone is hurting
❏ Sensitive—quick to pick up on the attitudes or feelings of others
❏ Focuses on people and their needs

Cautions:

- Beware of putting friendship ahead of telling the truth. Your friends need to know they need God's forgiveness and leadership.
- Make sure you don't get so involved in the process of building friendships that you forget the ultimate gift—helping your friends get to know Christ personally.
- Realize that you can get overwhelmed by the many needs your friends may have. Do what you can and leave the rest to God.

Suggestions for Developing and Using This Style:

❏ Be patient. This style sometimes works more gradually than others. Look and pray for opportunities to turn conversations toward spiritual topics.
❏ Look for—or plan—situations and events that will give you a chance to interact with new people.
❏ Practice explaining the gospel message so that you'll be prepared when you get a chance to share it.
❏ Team up with friends who have other styles that may be better matched to the personality of the person you want to reach.
❏ Other: _____

invitational style

Biblical Example: The woman at the well in John 4
Theme Verse: Luke 14:23

> *Then the master told his servant, "Go out to the roads and country lanes
> and make them come in, so that my house will be full."*

Personal Characteristics:

- ❑ Quick to include others in their activities
- ❑ Hospitable—enjoys making people feel comfortable and welcomed
- ❑ Persuasive
- ❑ Enjoys meeting new people
- ❑ Committed—strongly believe in the activities and causes they are involved in
- ❑ Sees outreach events as excellent opportunities for sharing Christ

Cautions:

- Try to avoid letting others do *all* the talking for you. Your friends need to hear how Christ has influenced your life and how he can make a difference in theirs.
- Think carefully about which events to invite your friends to. Ask God to help find ones that are sensitive to your friends' needs and interests while being clear with the message.
- Be careful not to get discouraged if your friends refuse your invitations. A "no" today may turn into a "yes" tomorrow.

Suggestions for Developing and Using This Style:

- ❑ When you invite your friends to an event, give them the details in writing (a flyer about the event, a handwritten note, e-mail). Whenever possible, offer to pick them up and do something together before or after the event.
- ❑ At events, put yourself in your friend's place. Ask yourself how, if you were your friend, would the event relate to your concerns and interests. Talk about those areas with your friend afterward.
- ❑ Offer helpful feedback to event sponsors. Give them specific suggestions for ways they could improve the event and make it more interesting or relevant to your friends.
- ❑ Be intentional with your conversations, using your discussion to challenge your friends spiritually.
- ❑ Team up with friends who have other styles that may be better matched to the personality of the person you want to reach.
- ❑ Other: _____

serving style

Biblical Example: Dorcas in Acts 9
Theme Verse: Matthew 5:16

> *In the same way, let your good deeds shine out for all to see, so that everyone will praise your heavenly Father.* (NLT)

Personal Characteristics:

- ❏ Humble
- ❏ Others-centered—thinks of others first
- ❏ Patient
- ❏ Sees needs and finds joy in meeting them
- ❏ Shows love through actions more than words
- ❏ Recognizes how even small tasks can be meaningful to others

Cautions:

- Remember that just as "words are no substitute for actions," "actions are no substitute for words." Romans 10:14 says that we must *verbally* tell people about Christ. Let your friends know Christ is the reason for your acts of service.
- Don't underestimate how important your service is. Your style will reach people who are the most negative and resistant to God. Acts of loving service are hard to resist and difficult to argue with.
- Balance your time and efforts wisely. Don't neglect your family or yourself as you serve others.
- Be patient—this style works over time.

Suggestions for Developing and Using This Style:

- ❏ Look and listen for even small ways you can show your friends they matter to you and to God. Even something as simple as picking up homework assignments for a sick friend could show how much you care.
- ❏ Ask God every day for opportunities to serve your friends. God will open your eyes to possibilities you may have missed. Be ready to follow where God leads, even if those leadings sometimes seem out of the ordinary.
- ❏ Be careful not to impose your service on others. Pray for wisdom to know where your service will do the most good.
- ❏ Team up with friends who have other styles that may be better matched to the personality of the person you want to reach.
- ❏ Other: _____

small group activity: *evangelism styles*

Directions

Form a small group with three other people.

1. Using the *Evangelism Styles Assessment* on pages 27–32 as a guide, explain your personal evangelism style to your group. Be sure to include the following information:

   a. One reason you think your style fits you

   b. Cautions you need to be aware of

   c. One idea for developing your style

2. Listen to the other people in your group to see what you can learn about their evangelism styles.

3. Choose someone to keep track of the time, so everyone gets 2 to 3 minutes to share.

the wrap-up

In this session you:

- Discovered your evangelism style
- Identified a step to develop your evangelism style
- Clarified your evangelism style using the *Evangelism Styles Assessment*

building relationships

PREVIEW

n Session 3 you will:

- Discover how to be more intentional in existing relationships

- Identify how to build new friendships

- Discover comfortable ways to start spiritual conversations

- Write down statements you can use to transition an everyday conversation into a spiritual conversation

building relationships

Friends and Family

People we _____ know

Suggestions:

- Let things flow naturally. You don't have to become a different person around your friends or try to change your friendships. Instead, _____ your conversations when you're together.

- Throw a _____.

- _____ first!

New Friends

People we don't know well, but would _____.

Four Building Blocks

- _____.

- Build on areas of _____.

- _____.

- Mention spiritual matters _____ in your relationship.

starting spiritual conversations

Three Approaches

Direct Approach

Usually takes the form of a question or statement:

- Do you ever think about _____?

- Where do you think you're at on your spiritual _____?

Indirect Approach

Begins with an everyday conversation, and then uses the topic of that conversation as a _____ to a related *spiritual* topic.

Invitational Approach

Transition from an everyday conversation to a spiritual conversation by inviting your friend to a _____.

Tips for inviting people:

- Offer to pick them up.

- Call to remind them.

- Pay their way.

- Do something together before or after the event.

individual and group activity:
starting spiritual conversations

Directions

For each of the situations on pages 39–40, imagine you are talking to a non-Christian friend—preferably someone from your *Impact List* on page 120.

1. Read each situation.

2. Write down a question or statement you could say to move the conversation toward a spiritual topic. Use the Indirect or Invitational Approach, whatever works best for you.

3. Complete as many as possible in the time allowed.

individual and group activity:
starting spiritual conversations

Situation	Possible Transitions
1. You and your friend are in a situation where it is natural to comment on beautiful weather, a spectacular view, a cool-looking animal, or some other wonder of creation.	You would say . . .
Sample Transition: "It's so awesome how God created so many different kinds of birds and animals."	
2. You are talking about the Internet with a few of your friends.	You would say . . .
Sample Transition: "I was in a chat room last night talking about creation versus evolution. It was really interesting. What do you believe about that?"	
3. You and your friend are talking on the last day of school before Thanksgiving, Christmas, Easter, or summer vacation.	You would say . . .
Sample Transition: "What are you doing for Easter? Does your family have any traditions like going to church for Easter service?"	

individual and group activity:
starting spiritual conversations

4. You and your friend are talking about which songs, TV shows, and movies you like and don't like.	You would say . . .
Sample Transition: "Did you see the music awards last night? So many people were thanking God for their awards. What do you think they meant by that?"	
5. Your friend tells you about a serious problem in his or her life.	You would say . . .
Sample Transition: "Would it be okay if I prayed for you? Prayer has made a big difference in my life."	

principles for starting spiritual conversations

1. Focus on your friend's _____ and _____.

2. Be willing to take _____.

3. Make the most of split-second _____.

Remember—Put Others First!

individual activity: *update your* impact list

Directions

1. Read the names you listed on page 13 to see if you still feel those are the people God is asking you to build friendships with. Write one of those names on the *Impact List* found on page 120.

2. Identify where the person is on the *Readiness Scale* on page 119. Mark their level, from 1 to 4, next to their name.

3. Fill in the following information for the first person on your *Impact List*.

   • List areas of common ground you have with that friend.

   • Review the transition statements you wrote on pages 39–40. Write down one or two you think you might be able to use in a conversation with your friend.

   • Determine the next step to take with your friend relationally and spiritually. You might want to look at the *Readiness Scale* on page 119 and the sample *Impact List* entries on page 120 for ideas.

4. Do the same for the other people on your *Impact List* (either now—as time allows—or later).

Note: There is a sample completed *Impact List* on the next page.

Impact List

Name: *Chris J. Sample*   Style: *Interpersonal*

The names on your *Impact List* will change as they become Christians or move out of your sphere of influence. This list should be an ongoing part of your evangelism strategy.

Remember to develop "no-strings-attached" friendships with these people. Let them know by word and action that they matter to you, regardless of whether or not they agree with the Christian message.

Name	Level of Readiness (1–4)	Areas of Common Ground	Conversational Transitions	Next Steps Relationally	Next Steps Spiritually
Jeff	2 (spectator)	• Same classes at school • Both like same sports teams • Both like playing football	"I'm reading a really interesting book about a Christian athlete. I think you'd like it."	1. Eat lunch together 2. Work out together 3. Watch playoffs together	1. Bring up spiritual topics 2. Give him Christian books about a professional athlete 3. Invite him to student activities at church
Steve	3 (skeptic)	• Neighbor • Same taste in music • Both like to debate issues	"I understand why you think some Christians are hypocrites. I've felt the same way . . ."	1. Spend more time together (earn trust) 2. Give him a CD to listen to 3. Invite him to a concert	1. Tell him my story 2. Research his questions 3. Invite him to a Christian concert
Betty	2 (spectator)	• Family member (cousin) • Same religious background • Both like camping	"My favorite thing about camping is looking up at all the stars at night. It always makes me think of how amazing God's creation is."	1. Call or e-mail more often 2. Talk about personal things on a deeper level 3. Plan a camping trip for this summer	1. Help her see the difference between going to church and having a relationship with Christ 2. Invite her to our student ministry 3. Ask what questions she has about God

the wrap-up

In this session you:

- Discovered how to be more intentional in existing relationships
- Identified how to build new friendships
- Discovered comfortable ways to start spiritual conversations
- Wrote down statements for transitioning from everyday conversations into spiritual conversations

what's your story?

PREVIEW

n Session 4 you will:

- Learn why your story is important
- Write out your personal story
- Practice telling your story in a safe environment

why your story is important

- Your friends are _____ in it.

- Your friends can _____ to it.

- It is _____.

how to organize your story

	Paul's Story—Acts 26: The Three Handles		
Handles	1 BC	3 MC	5 AC
Verses	2	4	6
Concluding Question	7		
Unifying Theme	8		

writing your story

BC—Before Christ

	Outline
1. What were you like before you came to Christ? How did it affect you?*	
Example: *When I was in junior high, my parents got divorced. I felt abandoned and angry. The last thing I wanted to do was trust God to lead my life.*	
*If you became a Christian at a young age, you can start with Question 2.	
2. What made you start thinking Christ could make a difference in your life?	
Example: *I began to see that I didn't have complete control of my life and that the anger I felt wasn't solving any of my problems. During this time my best friend really stuck by my side, and I saw how kind and different she was. I knew it was because she was a Christian. I began to wonder if Christ could make a difference in my life too.*	

writing your story

Meeting Christ

3. What was it that finally motivated you to trust in Christ?

Example: *When I asked my best friend about God, she told me that I mattered to God and that he wanted to help me. I knew then that I needed God, and that only he could take away the anger in my heart.*

Outline

_____

_____

_____

_____

_____

_____

4. Specifically, *how* did you receive Christ?

Example: *My friend invited me to pray with her. I asked Christ to forgive me and to be the leader of my life. I asked him to forgive my anger and all my other sins, and then to help me forgive my parents.*

_____

_____

_____

_____

_____

_____

_____

writing your story

After Christ

5. How did your life begin to change after you came to Christ?

Example: *It was so good to finally understand that God had forgiven me, that he would never abandon me, and that I could trust him. My life is no longer filled with anger.*

Note: For those of you who became Christians as children, compare your life now with what it might have been like if you had not come to Christ.

Example: *I grew up in a Christian home and gave my life to Christ when I was pretty young. Even though I don't have a story about how my life used to be crazy without God, I know God has made a real difference in my life. I've had some problems and hard times, and I've been able to rely on God during those times so that I never felt alone. My faith has given me a lot of direction and understanding I wouldn't have otherwise.*

Outline

_____

_____

_____

_____

_____

_____

_____

_____

_____

_____

_____

_____

_____

_____

_____

writing your story

After Christ	
6. What other benefits have you experienced since you became a Christian? Example: *Knowing I am forgiven and loved by God helped me learn how to forgive and love my parents again, and my relationship with them is much better. Whenever things get hard, I can read the Bible and get God's help and direction. I have a small group of Christian friends who encourage and support me. And I know I am going to spend eternity with God in heaven!*	Outline _____ _____ _____ _____ _____ _____ _____ _____ _____ _____
7. Concluding Question Example: *Can you relate to any of this?*	_____ _____ _____
8. Unifying Theme Example: *Looking for a way to deal with my anger.*	_____ _____ _____

story tips

Theme

- The theme is the part of your story that describes the biggest
  _____ in your life since you've known Christ.

Middle Handle

- Keep your description of this process simple, clear, and
  _____.

Conclusion

- End with a question or statement that evokes a
  _____.

Scripture

- If there is one key verse in Scripture that really fits your story, use
  it; if not, don't force it.

story tips

Language

- It's important to avoid using Christian phrases or church talk.

Length

- Keep it _____.

Sequence

- With practice, you will be able to start and end your story with any one of the handles, depending on the situation.

"Putting Others First"

- Earn the right to tell your story by first encouraging your friend to talk about his or her spiritual background.
- Emphasize the parts of your story that are similar to your friend's.

individual activity: *outline your story*

Directions

1. Look back at your answers to the six questions on pages 48–51 and circle three or four of the key words in each answer.

2. Write those key words in order in the column on the right side of the page. You will find sample answers on page 55.

> This is just a *first draft*.
> You will have plenty of time later to adjust it.

writing your story — sample

1. What were you like before you came to Christ? How did it affect you?*	*Parent's divorce*
	Felt abandoned and angry
When I was in junior high, my parents got divorced. I felt abandoned and angry. The last thing I wanted to do was trust God to lead my life.	*Didn't want to trust God*
*If you became a Christian at a young age, you can start with question #2.	
2. What made you start thinking Christ could make a difference in your life?	*Didn't have control*
	Anger wasn't solving problems
I began to see that I didn't have complete control of my life and that the anger I felt wasn't solving any of my problems. During this time my best friend really stuck by my side, and I saw how kind and different she was. I knew it was because she was a Christian. I began to wonder if Christ could make a difference in my life too.	*Best friend was a Christian*
3. What was it that finally motivated you to trust in Christ?	*I mattered to God*
	God wanted to help me
When I asked my best friend about God, she told me that I mattered to God and that he wanted to help me. I knew then that I needed God, and that only he could take away the anger in my heart.	*God could take away my anger*
4. Specifically, *how* did you receive Christ?	*Prayed be my leader*
	Forgive me
My friend invited me to pray with her. I asked Christ to forgive me and to be the leader of my life. I asked him to forgive my anger and all my other sins, and then to help me forgive my parents.	*Forgive my parents*
5. How did your life begin to change after you came to Christ?	*Forgiven*
	Never abandon me
It was so good to finally understand that God had forgiven me, that he would never abandon me, and that I could trust him. My life is no longer filled with anger.	*Trust God*
	No more anger
6. What other benefits have you experienced since you became a Christian?	*Love my parents again*
Knowing I am forgiven and loved by God helped me learn how to forgive and love my parents again, and my relationship with them is much better. Whenever things get hard, I can read the Bible and get God's help and direction. I have a small group of Christian friends who encourage and support me. And I know I am going to spend eternity with God in heaven.	*The Bible*
	Christian friends
	Heaven
Concluding question: *Can you relate to any of this?*	*Can you relate?*
Unifying theme: *Looking for a way to deal with anger*	

partner activity: *practice telling your story*

Directions

1. Get with a partner. One of you tell your story while the other listens and uses the *Story Feedback Checklist* on page 57 to write down any comments. If you are the listener, make sure to listen carefully and cooperate with the person telling his or her story.

2. After the first person has told his or her story, the listener gives constructive feedback on what worked well and what areas could be improved. Use the checklist to guide you.

3. Trade places. The storyteller becomes the listener, and the listener becomes the storyteller. Repeat steps 1 and 2.

partner activity: *practice telling your story*

Story Feedback Checklist	
Item	*Observations*
Three Handles: ❏ BC—clearly explained ❏ MC—was repeatable ❏ AC—clearly explained	**What worked well?**
❏ **Theme**—resolved a central idea ❏ **Conclusion**—asked for a response ❏ **Scripture**—did not overuse ❏ **Language**—avoided church talk (if not, what was said?) ❏ **Length**—was within 4 minutes	**Areas for improvement:**

the wrap-up

In this session you:

- Identified why your story is important
- Wrote out your personal story using the three handles
- Practiced telling your story

what's God's story?

PREVIEW

Session 5 you will:

- Learn the four parts of the gospel message—God, Us, Christ, and You

- Practice presenting two gospel illustrations

the gospel message

1. _____

    a.   God is _____.

         God is love; and all who live in love live in God, and God lives in them (1 John 4:16b NLT*).*

    b.   God is _____ (absolutely pure).

         But just as he who called you is holy, so be holy in all you do; for it is written: "Be holy, because I am holy" (1 Peter 1:15–16).

    c.   God is _____ (a good and perfect judge).

         The LORD *is known by his justice (Psalm 9:16).*

the gospel message

2. _____

   a.   We have all _____.

        For all have sinned and fall short of the glory of God (Romans 3:23).

   b.   We deserve physical and spiritual _____.

        For the wages of sin is death (Romans 6:23).

        (See also Hebrews 9:22.)

   c.   We are spiritually _____.

        *We are infected and impure with sin. When we proudly display
        our righteous deeds, we find they are but filthy rags (Isaiah
        64:6 NLT).*

        (See also Ephesians 2:8–9.)

the gospel message

3. _____

    a.   Christ is _____, who also became human.

In the beginning was the Word, and the Word was with God, and the Word was God. . . . The Word became flesh and made his dwelling among us. We have seen his glory, the glory of the One and Only, who came from the Father, full of grace and truth (John 1:1, 14).

(See also John 8:24.)

    b.   Christ died as our _____.

He personally carried away our sins in his own body on the cross so we can be dead to sin and live for what is right. You have been healed by his wounds! (1 Peter 2:24 NLT)

(See also 1 Peter 3:18; 2 Corinthians 5:21.)

    c.   Christ offers forgiveness as a _____.

God saved you by his special favor when you believed. And you can't take credit for this; it is a gift from God. Salvation is not a reward for the good things we have done, so none of us can boast about it (Ephesians 2:8–9 NLT).

(See also Romans 6:23.)

the gospel message

4. _____

a. You and I must _____.

But to all who believed him and accepted him, he gave the right to become children of God (John 1:12 NLT).

(See also Romans 10:13.)

b. You and I must _____ Christ to be our _____ and _____.

But if we confess our sins to him, he is faithful and just to forgive us and to cleanse us from every wrong (1 John 1:9 NLT).

But in your hearts set apart Christ as Lord (1 Peter 3:15).

(See also John 10:27; Luke 13:5.)

c. The result is a spiritual _____ by the Holy Spirit.

What this means is that those who become Christians become new persons. They are not the same any more, for the old life is gone. A new life has begun! (2 Corinthians 5:17 NLT)

(See also 1 Corinthians 6:19–20.)

partner activity: *presenting the gospel*

Do vs. Done
This illustration is a natural follow-up to the question "Would you like to know the difference between religion and Christianity?"

Narrative	*Outline*
The difference between religion and Christianity is:	
Religion is spelled "D-O." It is trying to *do* enough good things to somehow please God, earn his forgiveness, and get into heaven. This self-effort plan can take on many forms, from trying to be a good, moral person, to becoming an active participant in an organized religion—Christian or otherwise.	**Religion** • Is spelled "D-O" • Trying to *do* enough good things to please God
The problem is, we can never know when we have done enough. Even worse, the Bible makes it clear in Romans 3:23 that we can *never* do enough: "For all ... fall short of the glory of God." The "D-O" plan cannot bring us peace with God, or even peace with ourselves.	**The Problem** • We never know when we have done enough • The Bible says we can never do enough
Christianity, however, is spelled "D-O-N-E." In other words, that which we could never *do* for ourselves, Christ has already *done* for us. He lived the perfect life we could never live, and he died on the cross to pay for all of our sins. And now he freely offers us his gift of forgiveness and leadership for our lives.	**Christianity** • Is spelled "D-O-N-E" • Christ has *done* for us what we could never do — Lived the perfect life we could not live — Died on the cross to pay for our sins
But it's not enough to just *know* this. We have to humbly *receive* what Christ has done for us. We do that by asking for his forgiveness and leadership in our lives.	**Our Response** • It's not enough to just *know* this • We have to *receive* what Christ has done for us • By asking for his forgiveness and leadership in our lives
(At this point, ask a follow-up question like: "Does this make sense to you?" or "What do you think about what I just said?")	**Their Response** • What do you think about what I just said? • Does this make sense to you?

partner activity: *presenting the gospel*

The Bridge

"The Bridge" uses a simple drawing to illustrate the gospel message.*

Narrative	*Outline*	*Picture*
We matter to God. He made us, and he wants to have a relationship with us. *Write "us" on one side of a piece of paper and "God" on the other.*	• God wants to have a relationship with us.	
However, we have rebelled against God, we all have disobeyed him, our sins have separated us from him and broken off the relationship. *Draw lines by both words in such a way that they form walls around a large chasm, separating us from God.*	• However, we have rebelled against God and broken off that relationship.	
Most of us are aware of our distance from God, so we start *doing* all kinds of things we think are good so we can get back to God. There is nothing wrong with these things, but the Bible makes it clear that none of them can earn us God's forgiveness or reestablish our relationship with him. *Draw arrows going over the "Us" cliff. These signify our attempts to reach God that always fall short. Option: Write "Romans 3:23" next to the arrows so the person can see the biblical source for the illustration.*	• Most of us know we are separated from God, so we try to *do* things to get back to God. But none of our efforts work.	

partner activity: *presenting the gospel*

Narrative	Outline	Picture
Plus, the sins we have committed have to be punished. The penalty we owe is death, which is a physical death as well as a spiritual separation from God for eternity in a place called hell. *Add the word "Death" at the bottom of the chasm. Optional: Write "Romans 6:23" next to the word "Death."*	• The sins we have committed have to be punished, and that punishment is death.	
It looks pretty hopeless, but the good news is that we matter to God. In fact, God loves us so much that he did for us what we could never do for ourselves. He built a bridge so we could cross over to receive his forgiveness and restore our relationship with him. *Draw a cross so it touches both sides of the chasm. Optional: Write "1 Peter 3:18" next to the cross.*	• *But* God did for us what we could not do; he built a bridge that leads back to himself.	
He built the bridge by coming to earth as one of us and dying on the cross to pay the death penalty we owed. *Cross out the word "Death."*	• He did that by sending Jesus to die on the cross in payment for our death penalty.	
This is a picture of what the central message of the Bible is all about. This is what God wants each of us to understand. But it is not enough for us just to *know* about what God has done, or even to agree with it. We have to *act* on it. God wants	• It is not enough just to *know* what God has done. We have to *act* on it by admitting that we have sinned and by asking God for his forgiveness and leadership.	

partner activity: *presenting the gospel*

Narrative	Outline	Picture
us to move over to the other side. We do this by humbly admitting to God that we have sinned against him, and that we need his forgiveness and leadership. With our sins forgiven and our debt paid, our relationship with God is firmly established because we are immediately adopted into his family as his son or daughter. *While explaining this, draw a stick figure on the "Us" side of the chasm, then an arrow from the stick figure to the "God" side of the chasm, then another figure on the "God" side of the chasm. Optional: Write "John 1:12."* *At this point, ask them if the illustration makes sense to them, or if there is any part of it they would like to talk about. Finally, ask them where they are on the drawing and, if they seem open, whether they would like to move over the bridge by making Christ their forgiver, leader, and friend.* *Note: If they are not ready, it may be helpful to write in the four verses mentioned above and give them the drawing so they can study and think about it on their own.*	**Concluding Questions:** • Does this make sense to you? • Where do you think you are? • Is there any reason why you wouldn't want to cross over to the other side?	

partner activity:
practice presenting the gospel

Here you will practice presenting the gospel using either the "Do vs. Done" or "The Bridge" illustration. You will practice telling it as though you were talking with the first person on your *Impact List*.

Directions

1. Select a person from your *Impact List* on page 120. In 30 seconds or less, tell your partner what the person's first name is, how you know the person, and where the person is on the *Readiness Scale* on page 119. This will help your partner respond to you as the person on your *Impact List* might respond.

2. Choose the illustration—"Do vs. Done" or "The Bridge"—that you think would work best with your friend and present it to your partner. Partners, cooperate with the person presenting the illustration; do not try to make things difficult for them.

3. After the first person has presented the illustration, discuss together how each of you felt. The listener then gives feedback on what worked well and what could be improved. It's important to be honest with your observations so you can both improve your skills for communicating this life-giving message. If you need some help giving feedback, use the form on the next page as a checklist.

4. Then trade places. Repeat steps 1 through 3.

Here are some pointers for giving feedback:

*   For the presenter, talk about what worked well and name one thing you will do differently the next time you give the illustration.
*   For the listener, tell what you think was the strongest point of the presentation and give one or two suggestions for improvement.

Use the space below to draw "The Bridge" illustration.

gospel illustration checklist

Item	Observations
Which illustration was used?	**What worked well?**
❑ "Do vs. Done"	
❑ "The Bridge"	
Were the following four points mentioned?	
❑ God	
❑ Us	
❑ Christ	
❑ You	
Other points:	**Areas for improvement:**
❑ Was the presentation free of church talk? Was it easily understood?	
❑ Was what you needed to do clear to you by the end of the presentation?	
❑ Was the presentation within the 4-minute time limit?	

the wrap-up

In this session you:

- Learned the four points of the gospel message—God, Us, Christ, and You

- Practiced presenting two gospel illustrations

crossing the line

PREVIEW

In Session 6 you will:

- Practice telling your personal story a second time
- Identify the steps in leading a person "across the line" of faith
- Practice praying with someone to receive Christ

partner activity: *practice telling your story*

Directions

Pair up with someone you haven't worked with before. If you need to review your story, turn back to pages 48–51.

1. One of you tell your story to your partner as though your partner were the first person on your *Impact List*. (If you need to review your *Impact List*, turn back to page 120.) In 30 seconds or less, tell your partner the person's first name, how you know them, and where they are on the *Readiness Scale* (which you'll find on page 119). This will help your partner respond to you as the person on your *Impact List* might respond.

   Note: Those of you who will be playing the seeker should take it easy on your partner. You don't need to ask a lot of questions to confuse them or try to start a debate! Just pay attention and respond as though you are interested in what your partner says.

2. After the first person has told his or her story, the listener gives feedback on what worked well and what could be improved. If you need some help giving feedback, you can use the checklist on the next page.

3. Then trade places and repeat steps 1 and 2.

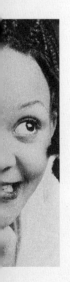

story feedback checklist

Item	Observations
Three Handles: ❑ BC—clearly explained ❑ MC—was repeatable ❑ AC—clearly explained	**What worked well?**
❑ **Theme**—resolved a central idea ❑ **Conclusion**—asked for a response ❑ **Scripture**—did not overuse ❑ **Language**—avoided church talk (if not, what was said?) ❑ **Length**—was within 4 minutes	**Areas for improvement:**

crossing the line

Assess Readiness

- Have you come to the point of _____, or are you still thinking about it?

- Where would you say you are _____ in the process?

- Is there any reason you wouldn't want to ask God for his _____ and _____ right now?

Pray

- Pray together, with you guiding the prayer by _____ your friend.

- Encourage your friend to talk to God and use their own words to:

  Ask for the _____ offered through Christ.

  Ask for God's _____.

- Give God thanks.

crossing the line

Celebrate

- Keep in mind that not everyone will react the same way.

- What matters is that your friend took a step of faith, not that they have any specific feeling.

- If your friend doesn't feel like celebrating, you should let them know that there are others who do—even in heaven! Luke 10:15b says:

  > ... there is rejoicing in the presence of the angels of God over one sinner who repents.

Take the Next Step

- Explain that they need to _____ with other Christians.

  - Get them involved in our youth ministry.

  - Invite them to church.

  - Introduce them to Christian friends.

  - Invite them to your small group Bible study.

  - Pick one day a week you could meet before school or at lunch time to pray and encourage each other.

- Encourage your friend to _____.

- Encourage your friend to _____ regularly, starting with one of the books of the New Testament.

- Help your friend understand how to relate to _____.

partner activity: *practice crossing the line*

Directions

1. Partner with someone sitting next to you. Using page 77 as a guide, practice leading your partner across the line of faith as though your partner were the first person on your *Impact List* on page 120. In 30 seconds or less, tell your partner the person's first name, how you know them, and where they are on the *Readiness Scale* on page 119. This will help your partner respond to you as the person on your *Impact List* might respond.

2. After the first person has practiced leading the other across the line, the listener gives feedback on what worked well and what could be improved. If you need some help giving feedback, you can use the checklist on the next page.

3. Trade places and repeat steps 1 and 2.

crossing the line checklist

Check those points of crossing the line that your partner included in his or her presentation. Use the space provided for additional comments.

Item	Observations
Assessing Readiness: *(check one of the following)* ❑ Have you come to the point of asking for God's forgiveness and leadership, or are you still thinking about it? ❑ Where would you say you are right now in the process? ❑ Is there any reason you wouldn't want to ask God for his forgiveness and leadership right now? **Praying:** ❑ Ask for God's forgiveness ❑ Ask for God's leadership ❑ Give God thanks	**What worked well?** **Areas for improvement:**

the wrap-up

In this session you:

- Practiced telling your personal story a second time
- Identified the four steps in leading a person "across the line" of faith
- Practiced praying with someone to receive Christ

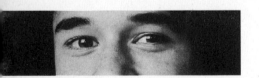

putting it together

PREVIEW

n Session 7 you will:

- Practice the steps of relational evangelism—from starting a spiritual conversation to "crossing the line" of faith

- List tips for telling people about Christ

partner activity: *putting it together*

Directions

This activity will include:

- Transitioning from an everyday conversation to a spiritual conversation. This is similar to what we did in Session 3. The difference is that in this case we'll assume you've already had several spiritual conversations with your friend and now they are ready to talk about the gospel and actually make a decision to follow Christ.

- Explaining a gospel illustration.

- Crossing the line of faith, which includes:
  - Assessing readiness
  - Prayer
  - Celebrating
  - Taking the next step (if you have time)

1. Pair up with someone sitting next to you. Choose a situation from pages 81–82 that you think you might face with the first person on your *Impact List*—or use your own situation. (If you need to review your *Impact List*, turn to page 120.) Use the checklist on pages 83–84 as a guideline for your conversation.

2. In 30 seconds or less, tell your partner the person's first name, how you know the person, where the person is on the *Readiness Scale* on page 119, and which situation you will be using. This will help your partner respond to you as the person on your *Impact List* might respond. Remember, for this activity, the person on your *Impact List* is ready to receive Christ. Begin the practice by saying the transition statement.

3. After the first person has made their presentation, the listener gives feedback on what worked well and what could be improved. If you need some help giving feedback, refer to the checklist on pages 83–84.

4. Then trade places and repeat steps 2 and 3.

partner activity: *putting it together*

Situation 1

You're spending the night at a friend's house when you decide to go to a party. You tell your friend that you told your parents you would call them if your plans changed.

"What's the big deal?" your friend asks. "No one will ever know."

"That's not true," you reply. "I'll know, and so will God."

"Get real!" your friend says. "What difference does it make? Do you think God really cares whether you call home or not?"

Sample Transition Statement: "That's what's cool about God—he cares about everything we do! God wants what's best for us all the time. Tell you what, how about if I show you how much God really cares?"

Or, if you'd like to use your own transition, write it here:

_____

_____

(Now go to page 83 to select the gospel illustration to present.)

Situation 2

You and your friend are talking about a classmate who was killed in an accident. The victim was driving home from a party you and your friend were at.

Sample Transition Statement: "It makes you think about how short life can be—and what happens after we die. Do you ever think about stuff like that? I used to think about it all the time and it really scared me. Then a friend told me how I could know for sure what happens to us after we die. It really helped me. Would you like to hear what I found out?"

Or, if you'd like to use your own transition, write it here:

_____

_____

(Now go to page 83 to select the gospel illustration to present.)

partner activity: *putting it together*

Situation 3

Your friend is dealing with some serious problems at home and doesn't know where to turn.

Sample Transition Statement: "I know when I was going through a tough time, I didn't know where to turn either. A friend told me God could really help me if I let him. And God really did help. He can help you too. Can I tell you how?"

Or, if you'd like to use your own transition, write it here:

_____

_____

(Now go to page 83 to select the gospel illustration to present.)

Situation 4

You're reading e-mail when a friend sends you an instant message, asking if you've ever checked out any of the X-rated e-mail ads for pornographic web sites. You message back that you've been curious, but that you delete those e-mail ads without reading them because of your commitment to God and to staying pure.

Your friend writes back, asking how you can buy into "all that religion stuff." You reply that you're not trying to act "religious," but that you do believe in God.

"What's the difference?" your friend writes back.

Sample Transition Statement: "Here's the best way I know to explain it. It's an illustration called 'Do vs. Done'..."

Or, if you'd like to use your own transition, write it here:

_____

_____

(Now go to page 83 to select the gospel illustration to present.)

putting it together checklist

Impact List Person (first name): _____

Use a transition statement:

❑   Use the sample or the one you wrote on pages 81–82.

Present a gospel illustration:

❑   "Do vs. Done"

❑   "The Bridge"

❑   Other: _____

Crossing the line:

1.   **Assess readiness** *(three questions you can use):*

❑   Have you come to the point of trusting Christ, or are you still thinking about it?

❑   Where would you say you are right now in the process?

❑   Is there any reason you wouldn't want to ask God for his forgiveness and leadership right now?

putting it together checklist

2. **Pray** *(three areas in which to prompt them):*

   ❑ Ask for God's forgiveness

   ❑ Ask for God's leadership

   ❑ Give God thanks

3. **Celebrate:**

   ❑ Acknowledge what has just happened.

4. **Take the next step** *(as time allows). Coach your friend on how to:*

   ❑ Get involved with other Christians

   ❑ Pray

   ❑ Read the Bible

   ❑ Relate to seekers

Feedback Section	
What worked well?	**Areas for improvement:**

tips for telling people about Christ

1. Don't give a speech.

   • Principle of "Putting Others First"

2. Give your friends as much as they can _____ right now.

3. Talk to your friends _____.

4. Be _____.

Advice for New Believers

• Don't overdo it.

• Be yourself.

• Don't underestimate what God can do through you *now*.

the wrap-up

In this session you:

- Practiced the steps of relational evangelism—from starting a spiritual conversation to "crossing the line" of faith
- Listed tips for telling people about Christ

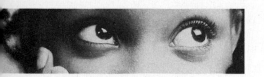

objection!

PREVIEW

n Session 8 you will:

- Identify common objections to the Christian faith

- Practice responding to objections

- List points to remember about approach and attitude when talking to others about Christ

video vignette:
answering objections, part 1

The questions raised in the video are listed below. A paraphrased answer for each question is provided on pages 90–96, which you will be given time to read later.

1. Why can't you just believe what you want to believe, and let me believe what I want to believe? As long as we both really believe in something, what's the difference?

2. As long as I believe in God, does it really matter what religion I follow?

3. How can you say that Christianity is right and all other religions are wrong? Isn't that narrow-minded?

4. How do you know that what you believe is true, and that Jesus really is who you think he is?

5. You keep using the Bible to answer my questions. How do you know the Bible is true?

individual activity:
answering objections, part 1

Directions

On page 90, you will find the first question Kevin was asked about his faith, followed by a shortened version of his answer in italics. After that, you'll see two other possible answers to the questions—not in italics.

1. Read the five questions in bold type on pages 90–96. Choose the one you think someone—preferably the first person on your *Impact List*—would be most likely to ask you.

2. Read the different responses listed under that question. Find the parts in each response that you would be comfortable saying to a friend.

3. Write down a brief outline of your answer in the shaded space to the right of the information. You will be using this information in a few minutes to practice responding to objections.

individual activity:
answering objections, part 1

On the following pages are the questions and objections raised in Part 1 of the video vignette. The answers given in the video are paraphrased and shown in italics. Additional responses to each question are also provided.

Video Vignette—Part 1	Outline
1. Why can't you just believe what you want to believe, and let me believe what I want to believe? As long as we both really believe in something, what's the difference? • *Believing something doesn't make it true, no matter how strongly you believe it. For example, imagine you went to take some medicine but accidentally grabbed the wrong bottle and instead swallowed something that looked like medicine but was really poisonous. No matter how strongly you believed you had taken the right medicine, you would still be poisoned and suffer the consequences. Your belief wouldn't change what actually happened, or the effects. It's not enough to just believe in something. You have to believe in* the right *thing and then act accordingly.* • This is true in all areas of life. Sincerely believing it is safe to cross the street doesn't help you if there's traffic coming. Thinking the speed limit is 65 when it's 45 won't prevent you from getting a ticket for speeding. And strongly holding your beliefs about God doesn't make them true. • What counts is not just believing, but what we believe in. We have to ask ourselves, "Is what I'm trusting in really	

individual activity:
answering objections, part 1

trustworthy?" Then we need to do our homework and find out whether it is or not. First Thessalonians 5:21 puts it this way: "Test everything. Hold on to the good."

For additional information read Chapter 1, question 4, in *Give Me an Answer* by Cliff Knechtle.

2. **As long as I believe in God, does it really matter what religion I follow?**

• *The question isn't whether or not you believe in God, but whether you believe in the* right *God. But because different religions teach different, contradicting things about God, all of them can't be right. For example, some forms of Buddhism don't even teach that God exists. Hinduism teaches that everyone and everything is part of God. Christianity teaches that God made everything but is separate from his creation. These definitions are all very different and can't possibly describe the same God. At some point, you have to decide which belief about God is really true, because they can't all be right. If you'll look into it like I did, I'm confident you'll discover the evidence clearly points to Christianity.*

• Other religions deny the biblical teaching that Jesus' ultimate mission was to give his life on the cross as a payment for our sins (Matthew 20:28). They also overlook the fact that of all the religions in history with leaders claiming to be prophets from God, Jesus alone backed up his claims by rising from the dead.

individual activity:
answering objections, part 1

- In both Old Testament and New Testament times, there were other religions in existence. None of them were considered acceptable alternatives by the biblical writers (Numbers 25:3–5; 1 Kings 18:16–40; 1 Corinthians 10:20).

  For additional information about various religions and sects, read *Cults, World Religions, and the Occult* by Kenneth Boa.

3. **How can you say that Christianity is right and all other religions are wrong? Isn't that narrow-minded?**

- *It's not narrow-minded if someone who has the credentials to know says it's the only solution. For example, if a pilot says the plane must land on that one narrow runway or we're all going to die, it's true that he's offering you a narrow range of options—but you'd be crazy not to take his advice!*

  It was Jesus himself who said, "I am the way and the truth and the life. No one comes to the Father except through me." Jesus gave his life to make it possible for us to be reunited with God. If there is another way to God, as other religions teach, then Jesus' death and resurrection were meaningless.

- It's also not narrow-minded if you've looked into it and found that Christianity proves itself in ways that other religions and viewpoints do not.

- Wisdom often leads us to follow a certain course of action over many other options. For example, when a family doctor prescribes a medication to help

individual activity:
answering objections, part 1

us get well, it's not narrow-minded to accept the doctor's advice, even though we know there are psychic healers and witch doctors who would suggest a different approach. The question is, whose credentials can we trust?

4. **How do you know that what you believe is true, and that Jesus really is who you think he is?**

- *Hundreds of years before Jesus was born, Old Testament prophets described what the Savior would be like so that people would recognize him when he came. They predicted where he would be born, what kinds of things he would say and do, and even how he would die. Jesus fit every one of their descriptions and fulfilled every one of their predictions. He also lived a perfect life, did miracles, healed people and, according to the eyewitnesses who wrote the Bible, rose from the dead after he was crucified.*

- Jesus' miracles were done openly and in broad daylight. They were witnessed by his followers as well as his enemies. The evidence was so overwhelming that his opponents never challenged *whether* he had done them. Instead, they focused on whether the miracles were *appropriate* or not. For example, when Jesus healed a man's withered hand, his enemies criticized him for doing it on the Sabbath day (Matthew 12:9–14). Their accusation proved that Jesus had actually performed the miracle, which was

individual activity:
answering objections, part 1

evidence that he was who he claimed to be: the Son of God (John 10:38).

- Jesus' greatest miracle—the one on which he staked all of his claims—was his resurrection from the dead (John 2:19–22). History shows that Jesus really did rise from the dead. His disciples, who doubted at first, saw and talked with him on many occasions after the resurrection. This alone can explain why they moved from fearfully hiding in the shadows to boldly testifying in public, even when it meant risking—and in most cases eventually *losing*—their lives. It was an appearance by the risen Christ that turned Saul, the enemy of Christianity, into Paul, the greatest Christian missionary who ever lived.

Also, Jesus' resurrection is supported by the fact that his body vanished from his carefully guarded tomb. The Jewish and Roman leaders would have quickly shot down the talk of a risen Messiah if they had been able to point to his crucified body and reassure the people he was still dead. But they couldn't, because he had risen, and there was no dead body to be found!

For additional information, see *The Case for Christ* by Lee Strobel, and *Know Why You Believe* by Paul Little.

individual activity:
answering objections, part 1

5. **You keep using the Bible to answer my questions. How do you know the Bible is true?**

- *In the drama, Kevin answers in two ways. First, he offers a book that will answer Ryan's questions about the Bible, and, second, he encourages Ryan to read the Bible for himself to see if God might speak to him through it. These are both good steps you could take to help your friend.*

- The first part of Kevin's response illustrates what we can do if we don't have an answer at our fingertips or if we don't have the time for an in-depth conversation. It's okay to direct people to reliable sources of information, such as books or teachers. It's also okay to tell them we'd like to study the question and talk with them more about it in a few days. Our friends are more concerned about getting a *good* answer than an *instant* one.

- The second part of Kevin's response is also important. One of the best ways to help someone see that the Bible really is God's Word is to get them to read it for themselves. Such personal exposure will help them rethink their stereotypes about what the Bible is like, show them how relevant its teachings are, create an atmosphere for the Holy Spirit to work in their lives, and point them to the truth. Generally, it's a good idea to direct people to the New Testament as a place to start reading. Also, be sure they have a Bible they can understand.

individual activity:
answering objections, part 1

- If there really is a God like the one the Bible describes, then it would be no problem for him to guide many different writers in different lands and different times to faithfully record his message. That, in fact, is what the Bible claims he did (2 Peter 1:20–21). An examination of the Bible itself bears this out. The consistency of the message from Genesis to Revelation is astonishing.

- The reliability of the Bible is strongly supported by history, geography, archaeology, and science. No other religious book enjoys this kind of broad support. Study in these areas has changed the minds of many skeptics who doubted the validity of Christianity, including Lee Strobel, one of the authors of this course. (You can read the details of what convinced him to turn from atheism to Christianity in his book *The Case for Christ*.)

For additional information, read *The Case for Christ* by Lee Strobel and the section "Questions About the Bible" in *When Skeptics Ask* by Norman Geisler and Ron Brooks. For questions regarding so-called contradictions in the Bible, see *When Critics Ask* by Norman Geisler and Thomas Howe, and *Encyclopedia of Bible Difficulties* by Gleason Archer.

partner activity:
responding to objections, part 1

Directions

Refer back to the question you just outlined.

1. Pair up with someone sitting next to you.

2. Tell your partner which question you chose from pages 90–96. Have your partner actually ask you that question.

3. Practice your response to the question while your partner listens.

4. Switch roles with your partner.

video vignette:
answering objections, part 2

The questions raised in the video are listed below.

6. If I became a Christian, wouldn't that mean I'd have to stop having fun?

7. Why would I want to be a Christian with all of those rules I'd have to follow?

8. Why should I become a Christian when the Christians I know don't act any differently than I do now?

9. If God can do anything he wants, why doesn't he get rid of all the evil in the world?

10. If God is so loving and kind, why does he let innocent people suffer and die?

individual activity:
answering objections, part 2

Directions

On page 100, you will find the first question Lindsey was asked about her faith, followed by a shortened version of her answer in italics. After that, you'll see one other possible answer—not in italics.

1. Read the five questions in bold type on pages 100–105. Choose the one from this set you think would be most likely to come up in one of your conversations, preferably with the person on your *Impact List*.

2. Read the different responses listed under that question. Find the parts in each response that you would be comfortable saying to your friend.

3. Write down those parts, along with any ideas of your own, in your own words.

individual activity:
answering objections, part 2

On the following pages are the questions and objections raised in Part 2 of the video vignette. The answers given in the video are paraphrased and shown in italics. Additional responses to each question are also provided.

Video Vignette—Part 2	Outline
6. If I became a Christian, wouldn't that mean I'd have to stop having fun? • *That depends on what you mean by "having fun." If you're talking about getting high, getting drunk, or having sex, then that's a pretty narrow view of having fun. The kind of fun you're talking about is external—it comes from the outside. It's amazing how much people will risk or give up for this kind of fun when the "buzz" from these things is temporary—and ultimately damaging. When it's gone, you're still left looking for the next "fix."* *The joy that comes from a relationship with Christ is internal—it comes from the inside out, from the deepest part of us. It affects every part of life. You can experience it in all your relationships and even when you're alone. Every day God is there to help you, so there's no need to go looking for the next "fix" to fill a void in your life. God has done that for me.* *And, for what it's worth, I have a lot of fun! I have a great time hanging out with my friends, playing sports, going to movies and concerts, and stuff like that. But it's the kind of fun I can still feel good about the next morning!* • The Bible tells us that God provides things "for our enjoyment" (1 Timothy 6:17). He's not anti-fun! But the Bible also makes it clear that we need God's wis-	

individual activity:
answering objections, part 2

dom and guidance to know how to use things appropriately, and to enjoy life in ways that won't bring regret later. That wisdom and guidance is available to anyone who will seek and then follow God.

7. Why would I want to be a Christian with all of those rules I'd have to follow?

- *It's probably more accurate to say that God gives us wisdom and direction, as opposed to a list of rules to follow and try to live up to. But because God created us, he knows what ultimately will protect us and make us happiest and most fulfilled. God's directions are designed to lead us to that happiness and fulfillment. Living under God's guidance actually gives us more freedom than restrictions, and following his lead means we don't have to worry about being slaves to what the world says will give us happiness and fulfillment. We can be truly free to be who we were made to be.*

- Being a Christian isn't about following rules; it's about trying to live like Christ lived. Christ's message wasn't so much "Don't do this and don't do that" as it was "Do what *I* do; follow *my* example."

- Also, when you start getting to know God better, you begin to realize that even his rules are good things! They're not designed to rob us of happiness. Rather, they're caution signs that say, in effect, "Not only is this wrong, but in the long run, it's going to hurt you too." For example, using drugs may seem exciting at first, but God wants to prevent the foolish

individual activity:
answering objections, part 2

things we'll do when we're on them, as well as the addictions and overdoses that might eventually result. Sexual freedom might sound great at first, but God wants to protect us from the loss of respect and relational damage that uncommitted sex brings, as well as the possible results of pregnancy or a sexually transmitted disease. God cares enough to warn us ahead of time, and to show us a better way.

8. Why should I become a Christian when the Christians I know don't act any differently than I do now?

- *Unfortunately, some Christians do act hypocritically. But it doesn't make sense to lump all Christians into that category. That would be like saying all teachers are clueless because you know of one who can't teach. Also, God doesn't make us perfect when we come to Christ, but he does promise to forgive us when we mess up. I hope you can see that while my Christian friends and I aren't perfect, God is making a difference in our lives. I sure can tell the difference!*

- If you base your spiritual decisions on the actions of other people, you're always going to come away disappointed, frustrated—and spiritually empty. People often use this argument as a smoke screen to keep from revealing their real concerns and issues with Christianity.

- It's interesting to note that when your friend complains about hypocrisy, he or she is in good company—with Jesus. No

individual activity:
answering objections, part 2

one spoke more directly or strongly against spiritual inauthenticity than Jesus did. In fact, he reserved his strongest words for challenging those who claimed to represent his Father, but who were actually giving him a bad name. So when your friend complains about these kinds of people, they're actually showing that, at least at this point, they're in agreement with Jesus. Maybe you should ask them if they'd like to go the rest of the way, and commit their life to him!

9. If God can do anything he wants, why doesn't he get rid of all the evil in the world?

- *This is a tough question I still ask myself. One thing that has helped me with it, though, is realizing that evil isn't just "out there" in the world. There's evil in people like me and you too. If God ever wiped out all of the evil in the world, he'd have to wipe out us as well. The Bible says that one day God will judge all evil. Until then, though, God is patient—he wants to give everyone a chance to turn away from evil and receive his forgiveness.*

- God created us with the ability to love and follow him or to reject and turn away from him. We chose to rebel against him and to follow our own desires. Romans 3:23 says that "all have sinned and fall short of the glory of God." Romans 6:23 explains that "the wages of sin is death." Knowing that we are all part of "the evil" that "God

individual activity:
answering objections, part 2

should get rid of" gives us a new and sobering perspective on things.

The Bible says that one day God will judge all evil. But right now, he is patiently giving us an opportunity to turn to him and receive the forgiveness and life that he offers (2 Peter 3:9).

For additional information, read *The Case for Faith* by Lee Strobel; the section "Questions About Evil" in *When Skeptics Ask* by Norman Geisler; and *The Problem of Pain* by C. S. Lewis.

10. If God is so loving and kind, why does he let innocent people suffer and die?

- *In the video, Lindsey responded very personally by telling about losing her cousin to leukemia. It illustrated the kind of situations we sometimes face that make us choose whether to turn to God or turn away from God. Lindsey doesn't claim to understand all the "whys" of what happened, but affirms that God was there to meet her in her pain. Lindsey goes on to tell of her realization that God understood what she was going through— God has watched his son, Jesus, being beaten and killed when he was innocent. This, Lindsey said, helped her open up to and experience God's comfort and support. Finally, Lindsey mentions that the Bible is the one book that is really realistic about the condition of the world in which we live.*

- This is a good model for us to follow when answering this question. Sharing your own experience of suffering shows that you understand and can relate to this difficult issue. Avoid giving "easy"

individual activity:
answering objections, part 2

answers to this very difficult question. Ask questions to find out why your friend is asking this particular question. Chances are, they have experienced suffering or the death of someone they loved and are trying to make sense of it. Be understanding and sensitive to their hurts. Often their need is for Christian care, not Christian answers. You can also point to the life of Jesus and how he faced the pain and suffering in his life.

- Point out that most of the evil in the world comes from people hurting other people—something God tells us not to do! God could stop us from harming each other, but he would have to limit or take away our freedom to do it. Needless to say, most people are not interested in having God limit their independence. God lets us choose which way to go, and the decision to turn from our self-centeredness and follow him is also our decision to make.

For additional information, read Chapter 10 in *Know Why You Believe* by Paul Little, and *When God Doesn't Make Sense* by James Dobson.

partner activity:
responding to objections, part 2

Directions

Refer back to the answer you just outlined.

1. Pair up again with the person you worked with earlier.

2. Tell your partner which question you chose from pages 100–105. Have your partner actually ask you that question.

3. Practice your response to the question while your partner listens.

4. Switch roles with your partner.

points to remember

Always be prepared to give an answer to everyone who asks you to give the reason for the hope that you have. But do this with gentleness and respect (1 Peter 3:15).

Approach

• Questions are not bad.

• Look out for _____.

• Answer the question, but then get back to the central message of the gospel.

• Use the Bible when appropriate.

• Ask _____ before you give answers.

Attitude

• When we respond to our friends' questions, we need to _____.

• It is important to show the person _____.

• Be _____.

the wrap-up

In this session you:

- Identified common objections to the Christian faith

- Practiced responding to objections

- Listed points to remember about approach and attitude when talking to others about Christ

course summary

Lost People Matter to God

Evangelism Styles

- Confrontational
- Intellectual
- Testimonial
- Interpersonal
- Invitational
- Serving

Starting Spiritual Conversations

- Direct Approach
- Indirect Approach
- Invitational Approach

Your Story—Three Handles

- BC—Before Christ
- MC—Meeting Christ
- AC—After Christ

God's Story—The Four Points of the Gospel Message

1. God

   - God is loving

   - God is holy (absolutely pure)

   - God is just (a good and perfect judge)

2. Us

   - We have all sinned

   - We deserve physical and spiritual death

   - We are spiritually helpless

course summary

3. Christ

   • Is God, who also became human

   • Died as our substitute

   • Offers forgiveness as a gift

4. You

   • Must respond

   • Ask Christ to be your forgiver and leader

   • Experience a spiritual transformation by the Holy Spirit

Crossing the Line

1. Assess readiness

   • Have you come to the point of trusting Christ, or are you still thinking about it?

   • Where would you say you are right now in the process?

   • Is there any reason you wouldn't want to ask God for his forgiveness and leadership right now?

2. Pray

   • Ask for God's forgiveness

   • Ask for God's leadership

   • Give God thanks

3. Celebrate

4. Take the next step

   • Get involved with other Christians

   • Pray

   • Read the Bible

   • Relate to seekers

Answer Objections

course evaluation

Becoming a Contagious Christian Youth Edition

Course Material

1. How did this course measure up to your expectations?

5	4	3	2	1
went beyond my expectations		met my expectations		did not meet my expectations

2. How much did you learn during this course?

5	4	3	2	1
very much		some		very little

3. How much of what you learned will you be able to use with your friends?

5	4	3	2	1
very much		some		very little

4. Would you recommend that others attend this course?

5	4	3	2	1
yes definitely		possibly		definitely not

5. What parts of this course were most helpful?

_____

_____

6. What parts of this course were least helpful?

_____

_____

7. What, if anything, should have been included in this course that was not?

_____

_____

Course Instructor

8. How much did your instructor's understanding of the material affect your learning?

5	4	3	2	1
very much		some		very little

9. How much did your instructor's motivation contribute to your learning?

5	4	3	2	1
very much		some		very little

10. How much did your instructor's interaction with the group affect your learning?

5	4	3	2	1
very much		some		very little

11. Comments:

_____

_____

_____

_____

_____

getting into a spiritual conversation— and keeping it going

When you're having a regular conversation, it is important to be thinking about how you can introduce spiritual topics. Generally speaking, the simplest way to do this is to ask a question, listen carefully to the response, and then follow up with another question. Listed below are topics that may come up in everyday conversations. Each topic describes a situation and then lists a response and questions you might use to transition into a spiritual conversation and then keep the conversation going. Following the example, there is space for you to write transition statements and questions you might use if these topics came up in a conversation with someone on your *Impact List*.

After you start a spiritual conversation, it's important to pay attention to how your friend is responding. Based on what you see and hear, you can decide whether to continue the conversation on spiritual topics or to move on to another subject. Body language and other signals will help you gauge which direction to take the conversation next. Sometimes you can just test the waters with a question or two about spiritual topics. Always be ready to back off, but also be prepared to have an in-depth conversation about Christ. Remember, God is at work and it's an awesome privilege to be used by God!

The Topic Is Sex

A few of your friends are talking about who they are dating and how serious their relationships are. When the topic of sleeping together comes up, one of your friends asks if you've had sex with the person you're dating. Here are three responses you could give that conclude with a question:

- "I used to think dating was all about having sex, but now I believe God wants me to wait. What about you—what do you think?"

- "God says he has a plan for our lives and part of his plan is to wait to have sex. Do you think God's plan could be right for you?"

- "You know I believe in God and that God knows what's best for me. Having sex is a part of God's plan, but not until I get married. Why do you think God wants us to wait? Do you think he knows what's best for us?"

What are some transition statements and questions you could use if the topic of sex came up in conversation with someone on your *Impact List*?

_____

_____

_____

_____

The Topic Is **Pressure and Stress**

Finals week is coming up and you're talking with a couple of friends about how hard it is to deal with all the pressure of school and thinking about the future. One friend turns to you and asks, "How do you handle it all?" Here are four responses you could give that conclude with a question:

- "I turn to God and pray to him. It helps me remember what's important, and how he is in control of my life. Do you ever ask God for help?"

- "What really helps me is just getting quiet and being still. It's in those moments that I'm reminded there's a God and he's in control of my life. Do you ever think about God that way?"

- "When I feel stressed, I talk to God or read the Bible. It really helps me. Do you ever talk to God?"

- "You seem like you're under a lot of pressure. Can I pray for you?"

What are some transition statements and questions you could use if the topic of pressure and stress came up in conversation with someone on your *Impact List*?

_____

_____

_____

_____

The Topic Is Getting Drunk or Doing Drugs

You and a friend who knows you are a Christian are leaving a party. Your friend has had a couple drinks. On the way home, your friend asks you why you never get drunk or do drugs. Here are three responses you could give that conclude with a question:

- "I get tempted sometimes, but I believe in God and I want God to be the one who is controlling me, not some drug or a drink. Let me ask you a question: Who or what do you want to control you?"

- "God says that he will give us lasting peace that sets us free. Does getting high give you that kind of lasting peace?"

- "You know I believe in God. Because of my relationship with God I don't feel like I'm missing out on something because I don't party. Do you ever feel like something is missing in your life?"

What are some transition statements and questions you could use if the topic of getting drunk or doing drugs came up in conversation with someone on your *Impact List*?

_____

_____

_____

_____

The Topic Is Death

You arrive at school one morning and find out three students you didn't know that well were killed in a car accident the night before. Everyone on campus is talking about it. Your friends are talking about heaven and what happens after you die. At one point someone turns to you and asks what you think about life after death. Here are three responses you could give that conclude with a question:

- "I used to be afraid to think about death. I still don't like thinking about it, but in a time like this I'm glad I know what will happen to me when I die. Do you believe knowing God makes a difference when you die?"

- "You know I believe in God and the Bible. The Bible says some sobering things about heaven and hell and what happens after we die. Do you believe there is a real heaven and a real hell?"

- "Listen, you know I believe in God. I'm not trying to preach to you, but I want to tell you what the Bible says we should know about death. Are you open to hearing it?"

What are some transition statements and questions you could use if the topic of death came up in conversation with someone on your *Impact List*?

_____

_____

_____

_____

The Topic Is Church

You are in a study group with three friends and your group has to finish a project over the weekend. You're trying to decide when to meet when one person suggests Sunday morning and then asks if that's okay. Everyone but you agrees. Your response is that you wouldn't be able to make it until later because you're going to church. They ask you why you go to church and if your parents make you go. Here are three responses you could give that end with a question:

- "My parents used to make me go to church, but now I like to go. The messages about God really help me with a lot of questions I have. When you have questions about what life is all about, where do you go to get your answers?"

- "I believe there is a God, and I want to know all I can about him. Church helps me do that. Do you believe in God or have questions about him?"

- "I want to get together with other students our age who are trying to do life with God. Do you ever think about God or have any questions about God?"

What are some transition statements and questions you could use if the topic of church came up in conversation with someone on your *Impact List*?

_____

_____

_____

The Topic Is Evil

You and a friend are on-line together messaging back and forth about the latest violent incident on a high school campus during which a student was killed. Your friend makes a comment about how much evil there is in the world and then declares that this latest event is proof that God doesn't exist—a loving God would never allow these kinds of things to happen. Here are three responses you could give that end with a question:

- "There's no denying that evil exists, but I believe that God exists too. Have you ever read what the Bible says about good and evil?"

- "I think God feels the same way we do about these things—I think it makes God angry and disappointed. Do you think every time something like this happens that it is God's fault?"

- "When I hear about things like this I think it shows how much we need a loving God. The Bible says we've all messed up—it's called sin. But because God is loving he wants to forgive us of our sins. Do you ever feel like you need forgiveness?"

What are some transition statements and questions you could use if the topic of evil came up in conversation with someone on your *Impact List*?

_____

_____

_____

_____

Remember, these questions are tools to help you to go further in conversations with your friends. When they ask questions, don't feel like you have to tell them everything you know about God in response. Instead, use these questions to draw people out and learn what *they* believe. Follow-up questions will help your friends see that you are interested in them and care about what they think. They will also help you develop enough trust to share your opinions on these topics. Use these and other questions like them to start great conversations!

write out your story

Readiness Scale

Level	4 Cynic	3 Skeptic	2 Spectator	1 Seeker	Receives Christ
Characterized By	Hostility. Not interested or open to being influenced.	Disbelief. May be slightly open, but bothered by doubts.	Indifference. May be open to ideas, but not motivated to apply anything personally.	Interest. Growing degree of openness; wants to know the truth and follow it.	
Suggested Approach	Ask questions to try to get at the reason for their hostility.	Ask questions to try to discover the reason for their doubts (misinformation, lack of answers to their questions, underlying "smokescreen" issues).	Try to help them think about matters of ultimate importance: why they're here, what their purpose in life is, where they stand before God.	Ask questions to find out the barriers that are keeping them from trusting Christ.	
Sample Question	"You seem pretty negative about spiritual things. Has something happened in your life to make you feel angry at God or Christians?"	"I can tell you have doubts about Christianity. Can we talk about some of your questions?"	"It's easy to get caught up in everyday life without ever thinking about what it all means. Do you ever think about where God fits into your life?"	"What would you say are the main things keeping you from committing your life to Christ?"	
Your Response	Listen carefully, empathize where possible; try to help them reconsider their response to whatever happened.	Listen carefully, try to answer their questions, help them start actively looking at the evidence for Christianity.	Encourage them to not wait for tough times or tragedy to think about spiritual issues. Share a personal experience that illustrates why following Christ makes sense now, as well as for eternity.	Correct any misunderstandings they may have, answer any questions, show them that the benefits of following Christ far outweigh any costs, move them toward crossing the line of faith.	

Notes

- When you think about where your friends are on this scale, think about how open they are to your influence—to listening to what you have to say and allowing it to make a difference in their life. Just because a friend is open to talking about spiritual issues doesn't necessarily mean they are open to changing their views or their life because of it.
- It is possible for a person to do religious things—going to church, saying prayers, observing holidays—and still not have a personal relationship with Christ. A person may be very religious but still be a cynic, skeptic, spectator, or seeker because they have not yet asked Jesus to be their Forgiver and Leader.
- People do not necessarily progress through each of these areas; they can move from any one of them to any other, including directly to receiving Christ.

Impact List   Name: _____   Style: _____

The names on your *Impact List* will change as they become Christians or move out of your sphere of influence. This list should be an ongoing part of your evangelism strategy.

Remember to develop "no-strings-attached" friendships with these people. Let them know by word and action that they matter to you, regardless of whether or not they agree with the Christian message.

Name	Level of Readiness (1–4)	Areas of Common Ground	Conversational Transitions	Next Steps Relationally	Next Steps Spiritually
			1. 2. 3.	1. 2. 3.	1. 2. 3.
			1. 2. 3.	1. 2. 3.	1. 2. 3.
			1. 2. 3.	1. 2. 3.	1. 2. 3.

bibliography

evangelism

Becoming a Contagious Christian, Bill Hybels and Mark Mittelberg, Zondervan, 1994 (the companion book to this course).

Building a Contagious Church, Mark Mittelberg, Zondervan, 2000.

Don't Check Your Brains at the Door, Josh McDowell, Word, 1992.

How to Give Away Your Faith, Paul Little, InterVarsity Press, 1966.

Inside the Mind of Unchurched Harry and Mary, Lee Strobel, Zondervan, 1993.

Inside the Soul of a New Generation, Tim Celek and Dieter Zander, Zondervan, 1996.

Lifestyle Evangelism, Joseph Aldrich, Multnomah, 1981.

Living Proof, Jim Petersen, NavPress, 1989.

Out of the Saltshaker, Rebecca Manley Pippert, InterVarsity, 1979.

resources for seekers

Basic Christianity, John R. W. Stott, InterVarsity Press, 1971.

The Case for Christ, Lee Strobel, Zondervan, 1998.

The Case for Faith, Lee Strobel, Zondervan, 2000.

Christianity 101, Gilbert Bilezikian, Zondervan, 1993.

The God You're Looking For, Bill Hybels, Thomas Nelson, 1997.

Give Me an Answer, Cliff Knechtle, InterVarsity Press, 1986.

Know Why You Believe, Paul Little, InterVarsity Press, 1988.

More Than a Carpenter, Josh McDowell, Tyndale, 1977.

Reason to Believe, R. C. Sproul, Zondervan, 1970.

The Reason Why, Robert Laidlaw, Zondervan, 1970.

Tough Questions Series, Garry Poole and Judson Poling, Zondervan, 1998.

The Journey Bible, Zondervan, 1996.

What Jesus Would Say, Lee Strobel, Zondervan, 1994.

Willow Creek Association

VISION,   TRAINING,   RESOURCES,

FOR PREVAILING CHURCHES

This resource was created to serve you and to help you in building a local church that prevails! It is just one of many Willow Creek Resources copublished by the Willow Creek Association and Zondervan Publishing House.

Since 1992, the Willow Creek Association (WCA) has been linking like-minded, action-oriented churches with each other and with strategic vision, training, and resources. Now a worldwide network of over five thousand churches from more than eighty denominations, the WCA works to equip Member Churches and others with the tools needed to build prevailing churches. Our desire is to inspire, equip, and encourage Christian leaders to build biblically functioning churches that reach increasing numbers of unchurched people, not just with innovations from Willow Creek Community Church in South Barrington, Illinois, but from any church in the world that has experienced God-given breakthroughs.

Willow Creek Conferences

In the past year, more than 65,000 local church leaders, staff, and volunteers—from WCA Member Churches and others—attended one of our conferences or training events.

Conferences offered on the Willow Creek campus in South Barrington, Illinois, include:

Prevailing Church Conference—Foundational training for staff and volunteers working to build a prevailing local church; offered twice each year.

Prevailing Church Workshops—More than fifty workshops cover seven topic areas that represent key characteristics of a prevailing church; offered twice each year.

Promiseland Conference—Children's ministries; infant through fifth grade.

Prevailing Youth Ministries Conference—Junior and senior high ministries.

Arts Conference—Vision and training for Christian artists using their gifts in the ministries of local churches.

Leadership Summit—Envisioning and equipping Christians with leadership gifts and responsibilities; broadcast live via satellite to sixteen cities.

Contagious Evangelism Conference—Encouragement and training for churches and church leaders who want to be strategic in reaching lost people for Christ.

Small Groups Conference—Exploring how small groups can play a key role in developing authentic Christian community that leads to spiritual transformation.

Prevailing Church Regional Workshops

Each year the WCA team leads seven, two-day training events in cities across the United States. Workshops are offered in topic areas including leadership, next-generation ministries, small groups, arts and worship, evangelism, spiritual gifts, financial stewardship, and spiritual formation. These events make quality training more accessible and affordable to larger groups of staff and volunteers.

Willow Creek Resources

Churches can look to Willow Creek Resources for a trusted channel of ministry tools in areas of leadership, evangelism, spiritual gifts, small groups, drama, contemporary music, financial stewardship, spiritual transformation, and more. For ordering information, call 800-570-9812 or visit www.willowcreek.com.

WCA Membership

Membership in the Willow Creek Association as well as attendance at WCA Conferences is for churches, ministries, and leaders who hold to a historic, orthodox understanding of biblical Christianity. The annual church membership fee of $249 provides discounts for your entire team on all conferences and Willow Creek Resources, networking opportunities with other outreach-oriented churches, a bimonthly newsletter, a subscription to *Defining Moments* monthly audio journal, and more.

WillowNet (www.willowcreek.com)

This internet service provides you with access to hundreds of Willow Creek messages, drama scripts, songs, videos, and multimedia suggestions. The system allows you to sort through these elements and download them for a fee.

Our website also provides detailed information on the Willow Creek Association, Willow Creek Community Church, WCA Membership, conferences, training events, resources, and more.

Willow Creek Association
P.O. Box 3188
Barrington, IL 60011-3188
Phone: 800-570-9812
Fax: 888-922-0035
Web: www.willowcreek.com

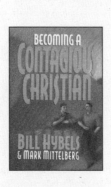

Building a Contagious Church

MARK MITTELBERG
WITH CONTRIBUTIONS BY BILL HYBELS

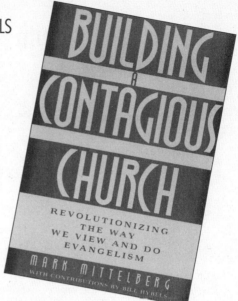

Building a Contagious Church offers a proven, six-stage process to help your church become highly contagious—regardless of its size, location, or style of worship. This powerful book also expands on the six styles of evangelism presented in *Becoming a Contagious Christian* and shows how the styles can be expressed at a broader ministry level. Loaded with stories, ideas, and examples from scores of churches, this book provides a compelling vision of a highly evangelistic church, as well as the specific steps it takes to get there.

Hardcover 0-310-22149-8

Pick up a copy today at your favorite bookstore!

GRAND RAPIDS, MICHIGAN 49530

WILLOW
CREEK
RESOURCES

The Case for Faith

LEE STROBEL

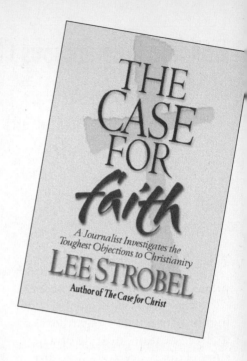

In this much anticipated follow-up to *The Case for Christ,* award-winning reporter Lee Strobel tackles eight obstacles to faith. These include questions like, "If God is love, then what about all of the suffering in the world?" Or, "If Jesus is the door to heaven, then what about the millions who have never heard of him?"

The Case for Faith is for those who may be feeling attracted to Jesus but who are faced with formidable intellectual barriers. For Christians, it will deepen their convictions and give them fresh confidence in discussing Christianity with even their most skeptical friends.

Hardcover	0-310-22015-7
Softcover	0-310-23469-7
Evangelism Pack	0-310-23508-1
Mass Market 6-pack	0-310-23509-X
Audio Pages® Abridged Cassettes	0-310-23475-1

Pick up a copy today at your favorite bookstore!

GRAND RAPIDS, MICHIGAN 49530

WILLOW CREEK RESOURCES

The Case for Christ —
Student Edition

LEE STROBEL WITH JANE VOGEL

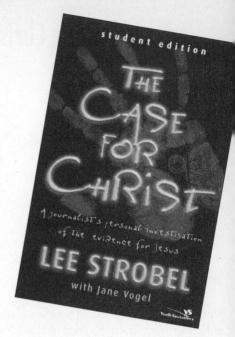

In *The Case for Christ—Student Edition*, students will accompany Strobel on his fascinating journey of discovery as he unearths convincing evidence that faith in Jesus of Nazareth is based not on wishful thinking or legend but on solid historical facts. Through this creative, fast-paced, and high-energy book, students will be pointed toward Christ as the answer for living.

Softcover 0-310-23484-0

Pick up a copy today at your favorite bookstore!

GRAND RAPIDS, MICHIGAN 49530